Relaxing Hawaiian Scenes:
An Adult Coloring Book

by

Stephen Jorgensen
(artist)

published by
CyberSuccess Publishing
Honolulu, Hawaii

i

This book is a coloring book for adults. It is more complicated than a child's coloring book with smaller and finer details. You have to concentrate to color in all the small shapes. That makes it an ideal method to clear your mind of many negative thoughts and it helps you relieve stress. Coloring will reduce anxiety, and help you focus and will bring you more mindfulness. It is therapeutic.

Plus, this coloring book will bring the beauty of Hawaii into your life. The next best thing to actually going there. All the work here is by the Hawaiian artist Stephen E Jorgensen. He has over 200 other works of beautiful Hawaiian art available on his Etsy website. Most of his work is large canvas wall hangings, some of which are reduced to coloring pages in this book. See these at hawaiiseascapes.etsy.com

ISBN-13: 978-1539504801

ISBN-10: 1539504808

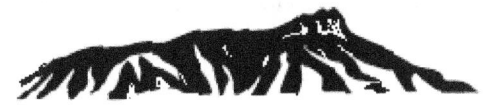

Relaxing Hawaiian Scenes:
An Adult Coloring Book

Many of the pictures here seem like just a jumble of shapes as they are outlines of slightly different painted colors in the originals. You have to look at the full color reproductions shown on the front and back covers to see what color the shapes are and what the result should look like. You don't have to use the exact same colors but the images on the covers will show you where the fish ends and the coral begins, or where the flower petal ends and the leaves begins, and so on.

Many of the colors are just slightly different, so it is best to used a large selection of colored pencils to be able to find an appropriate color, and it helps to "layer" two different colors to get a better match. For instance, coloring a purple over a red will give a darker more scarlet red.

All the coloring pages are one side only, so no bleed-through will mess up a drawing on the opposite side of the page if you do use color marking pens.

Enjoy your coloring.

This Hawaiian Coloring Therapy
Will relax you.

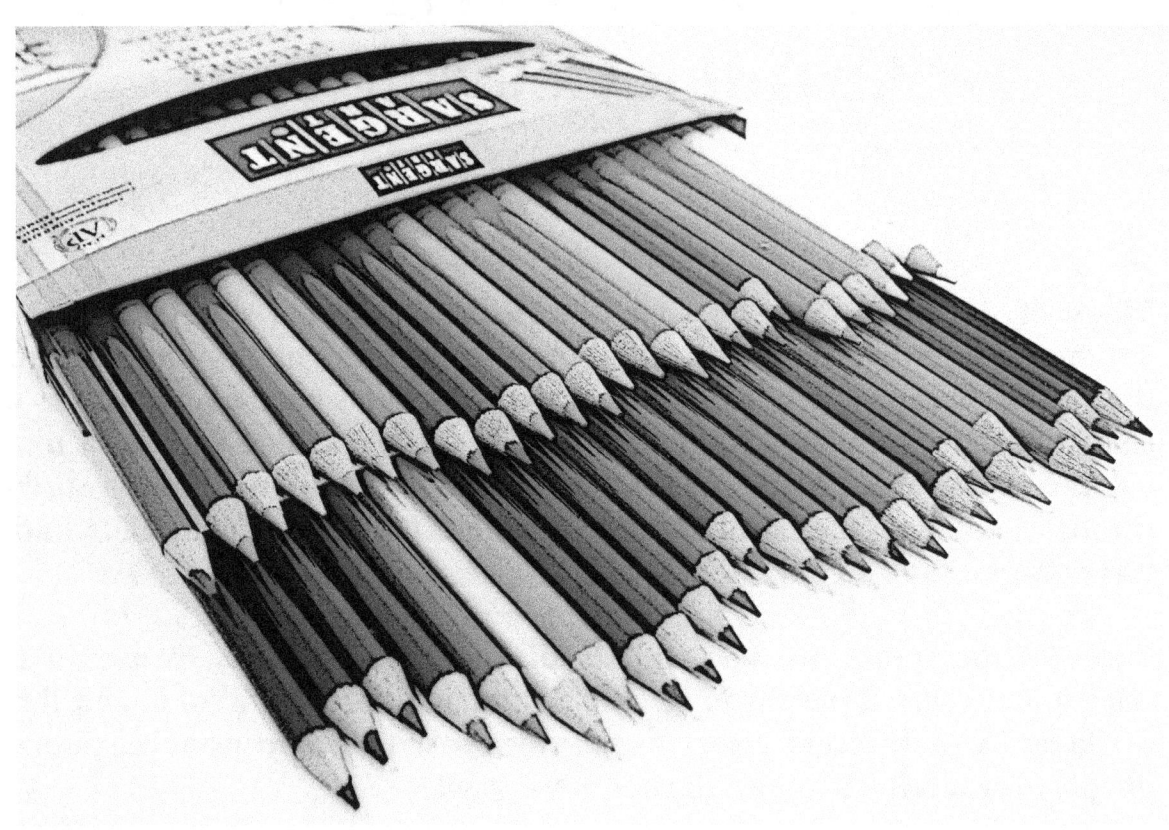

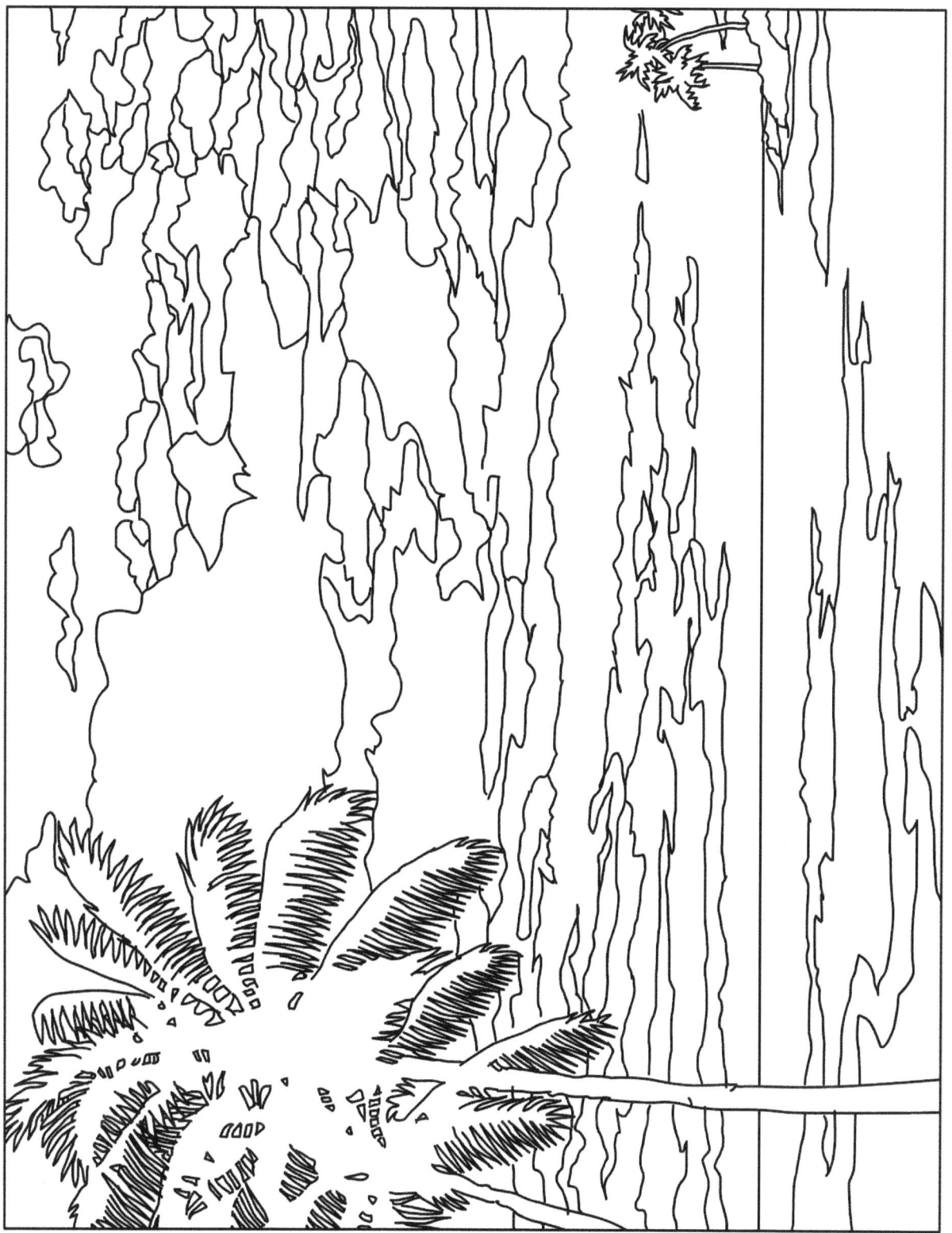

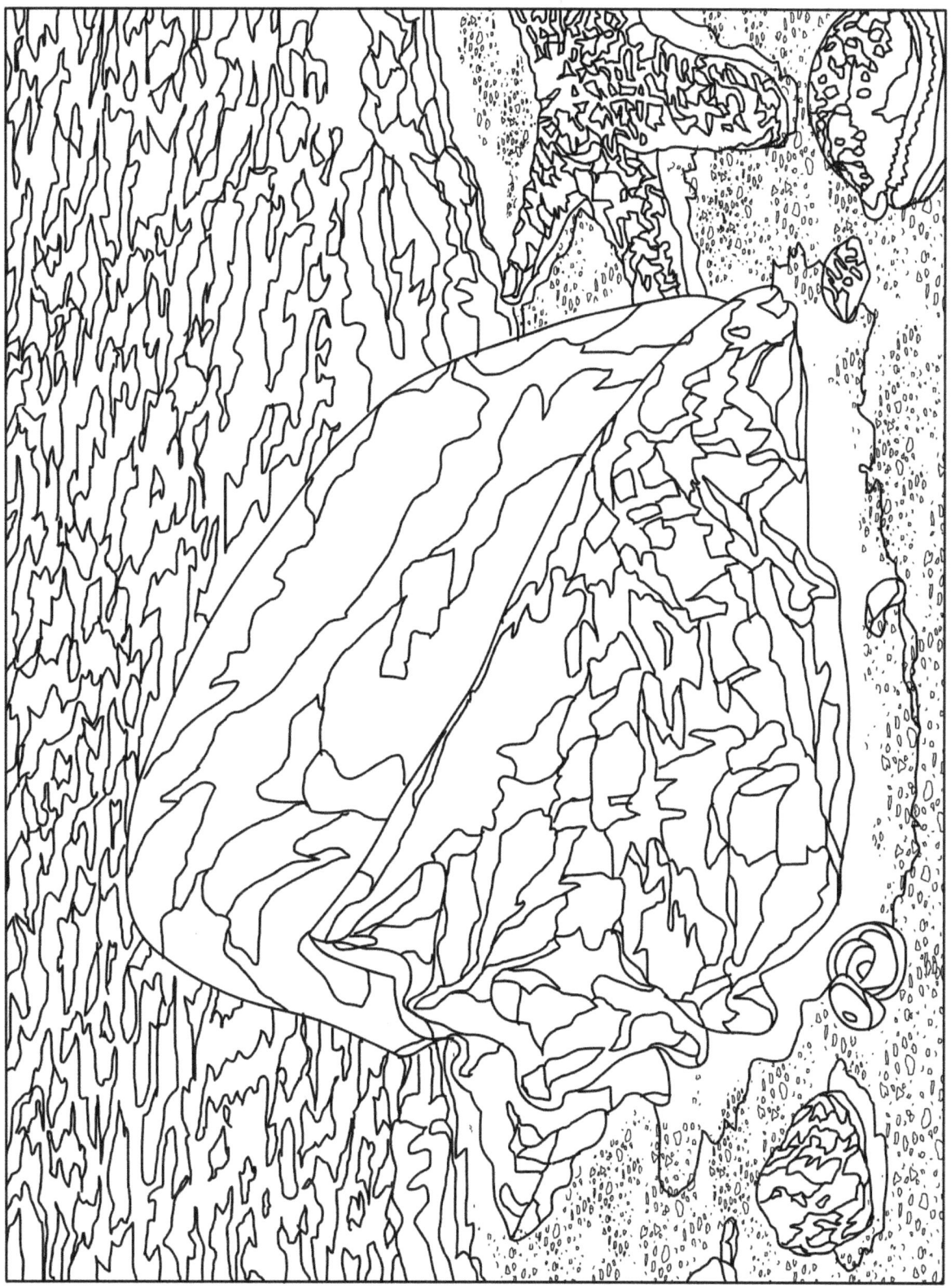

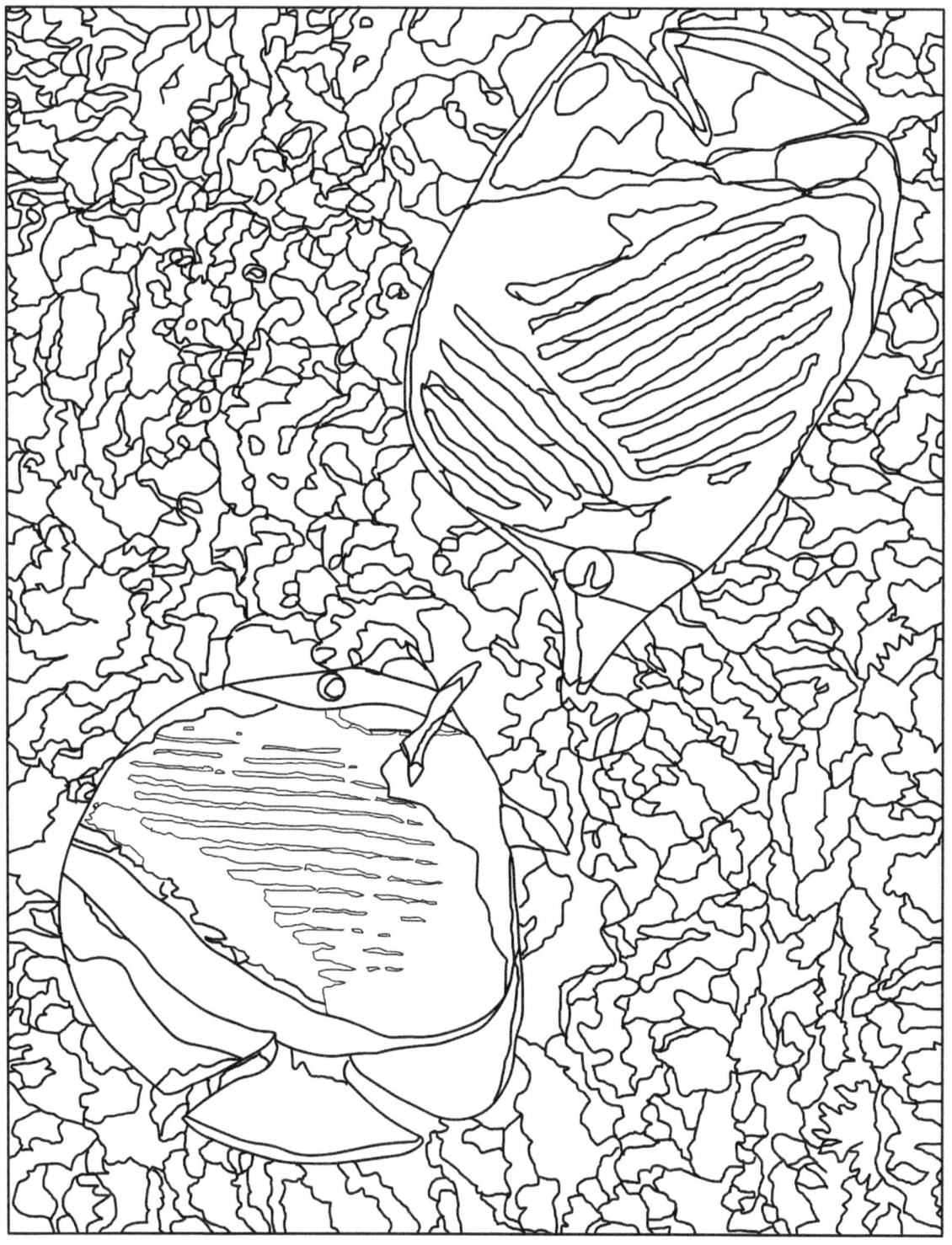

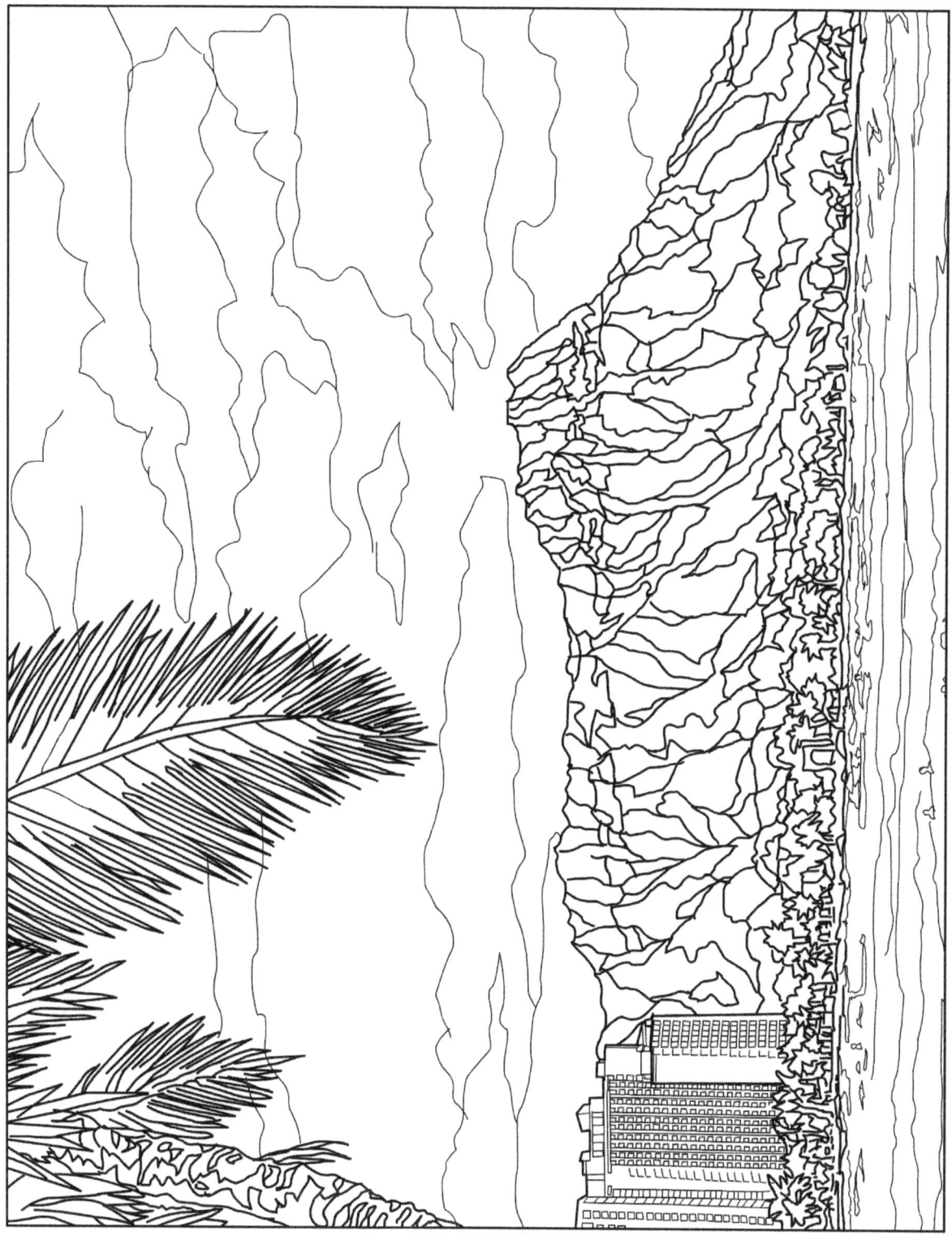

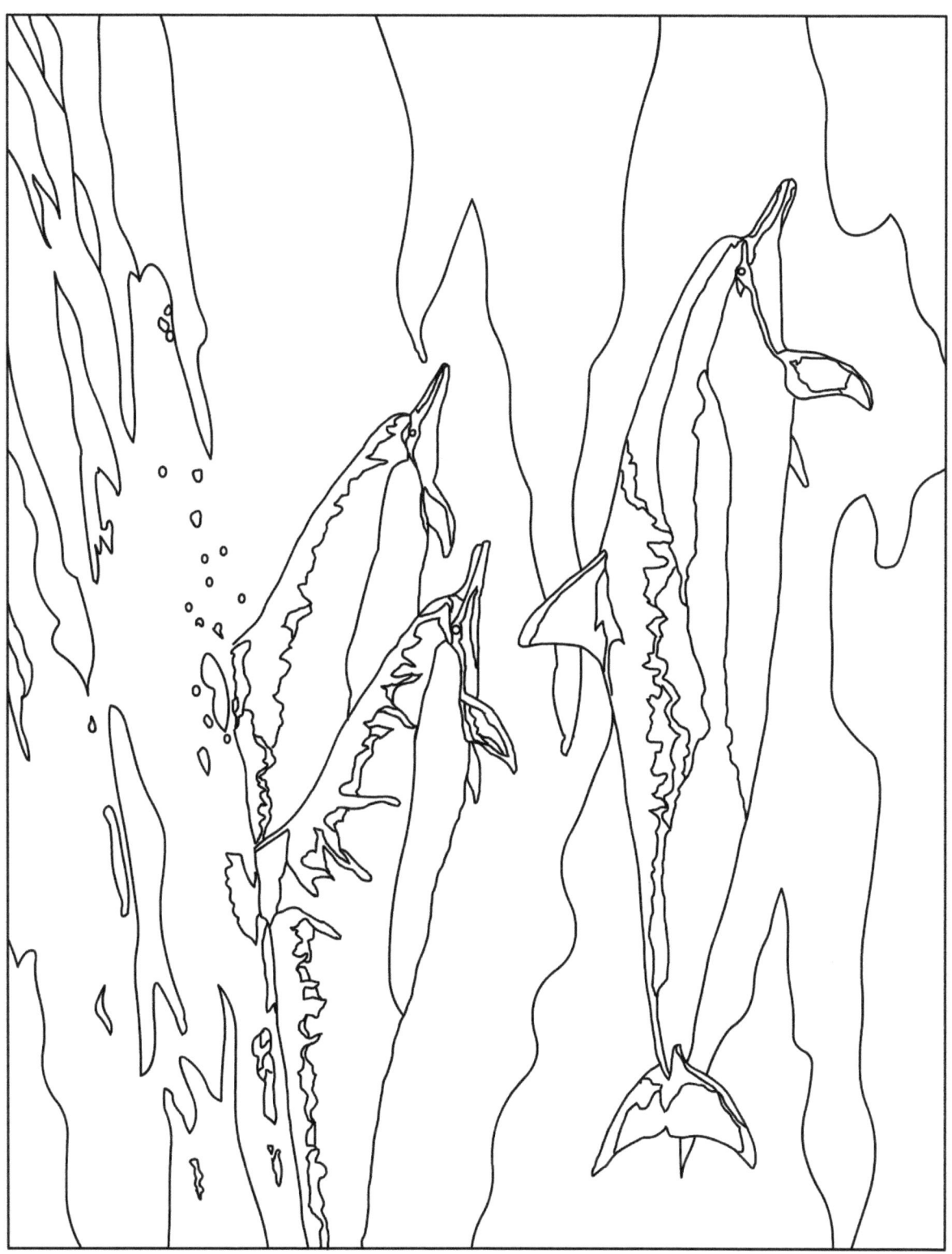

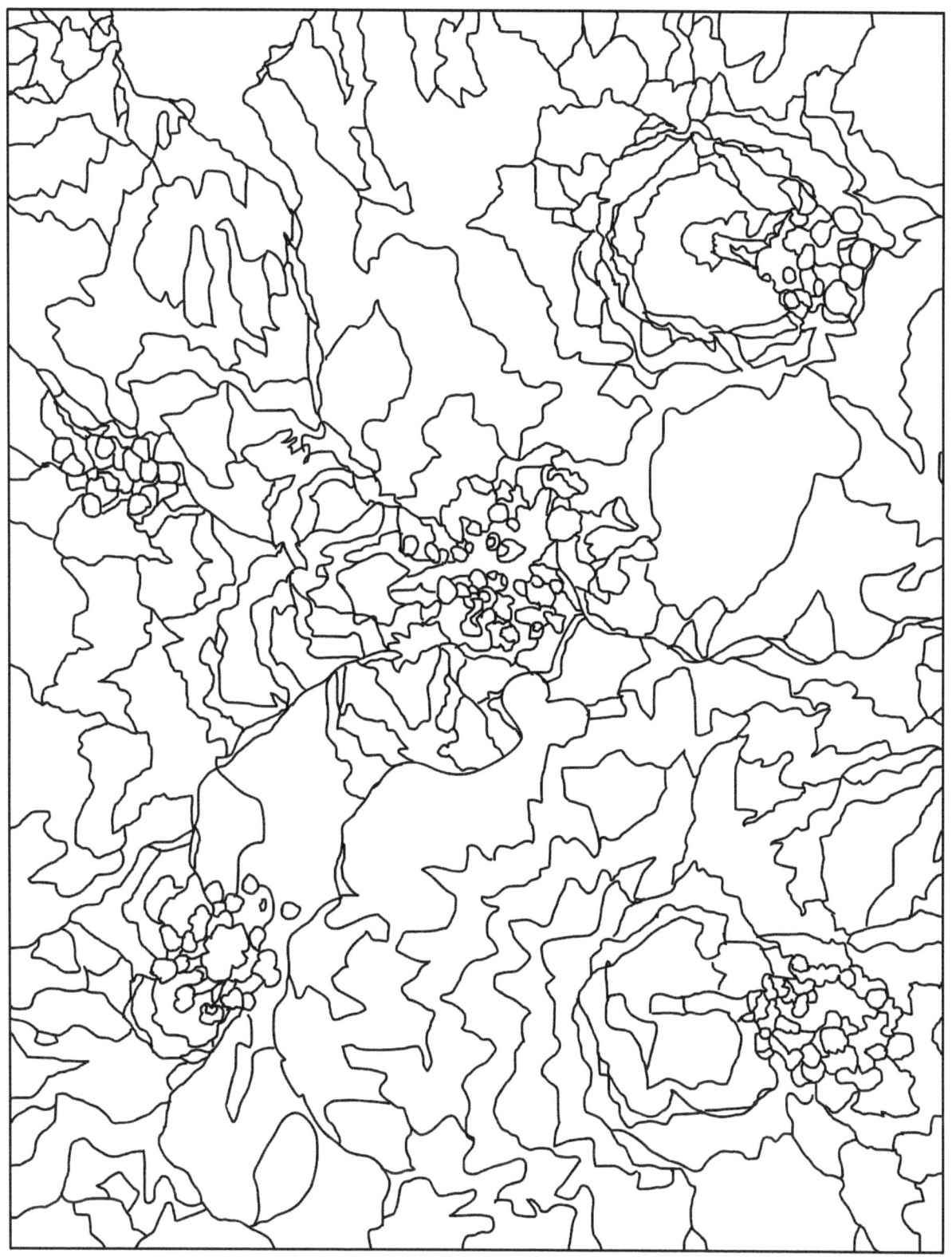

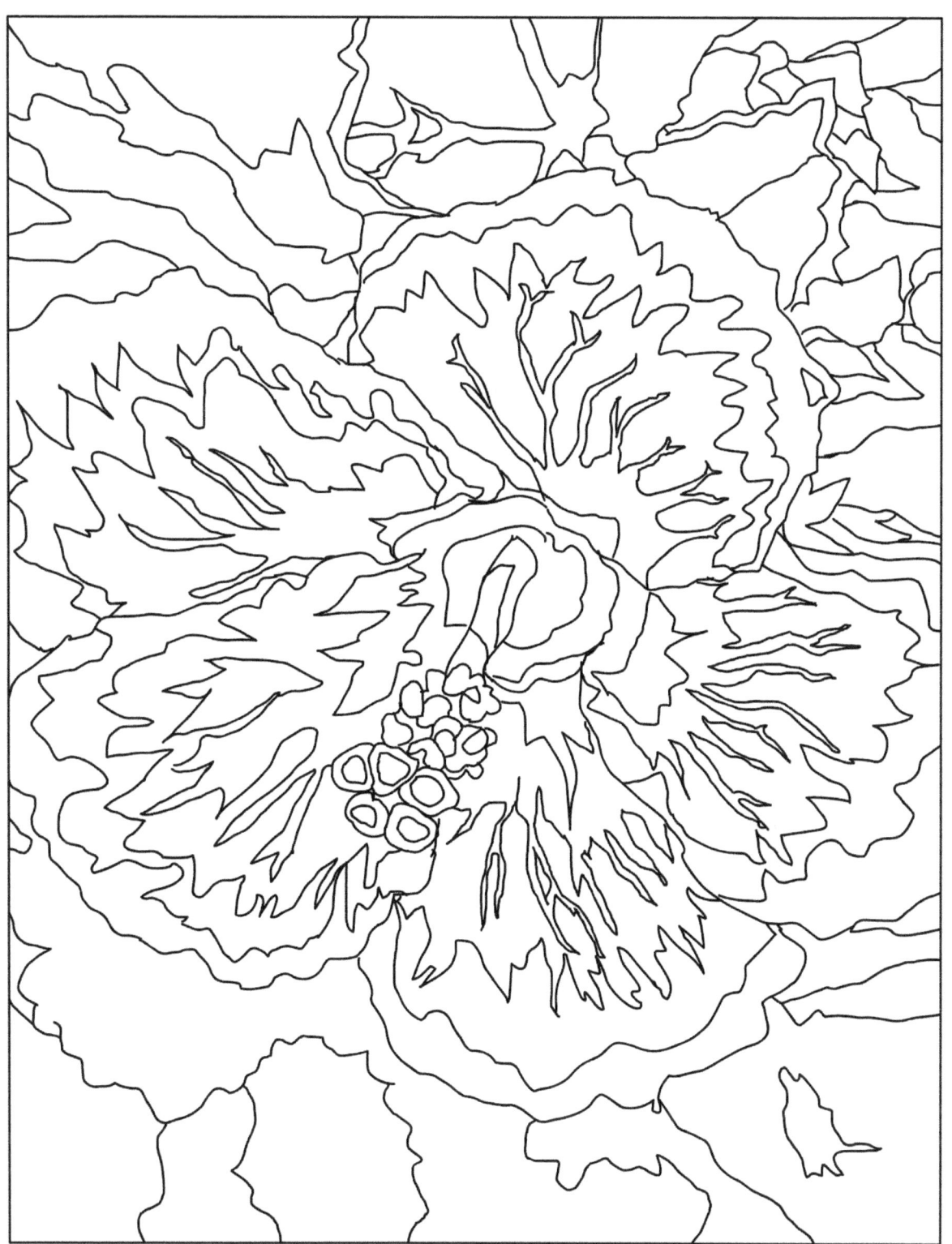

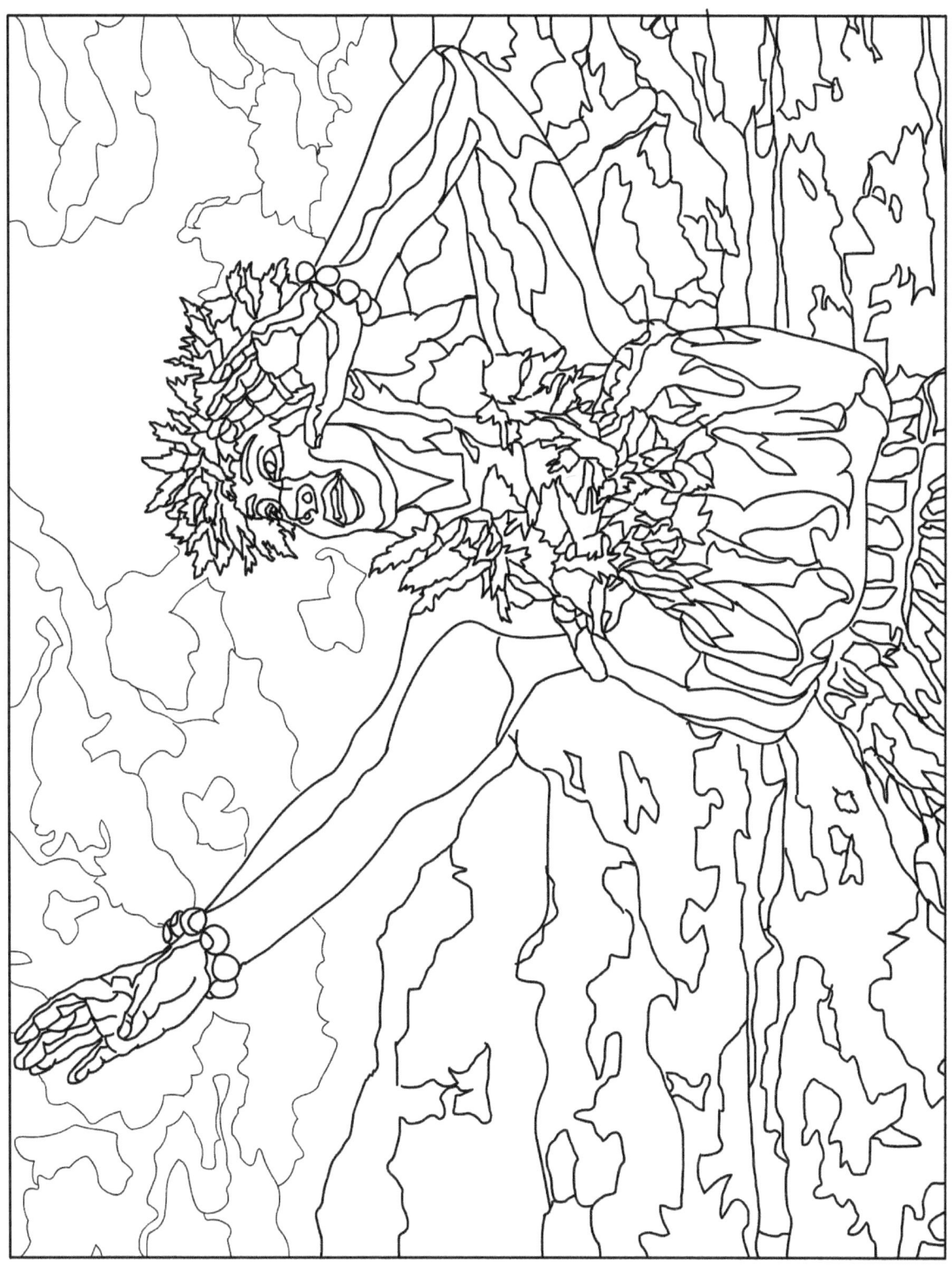

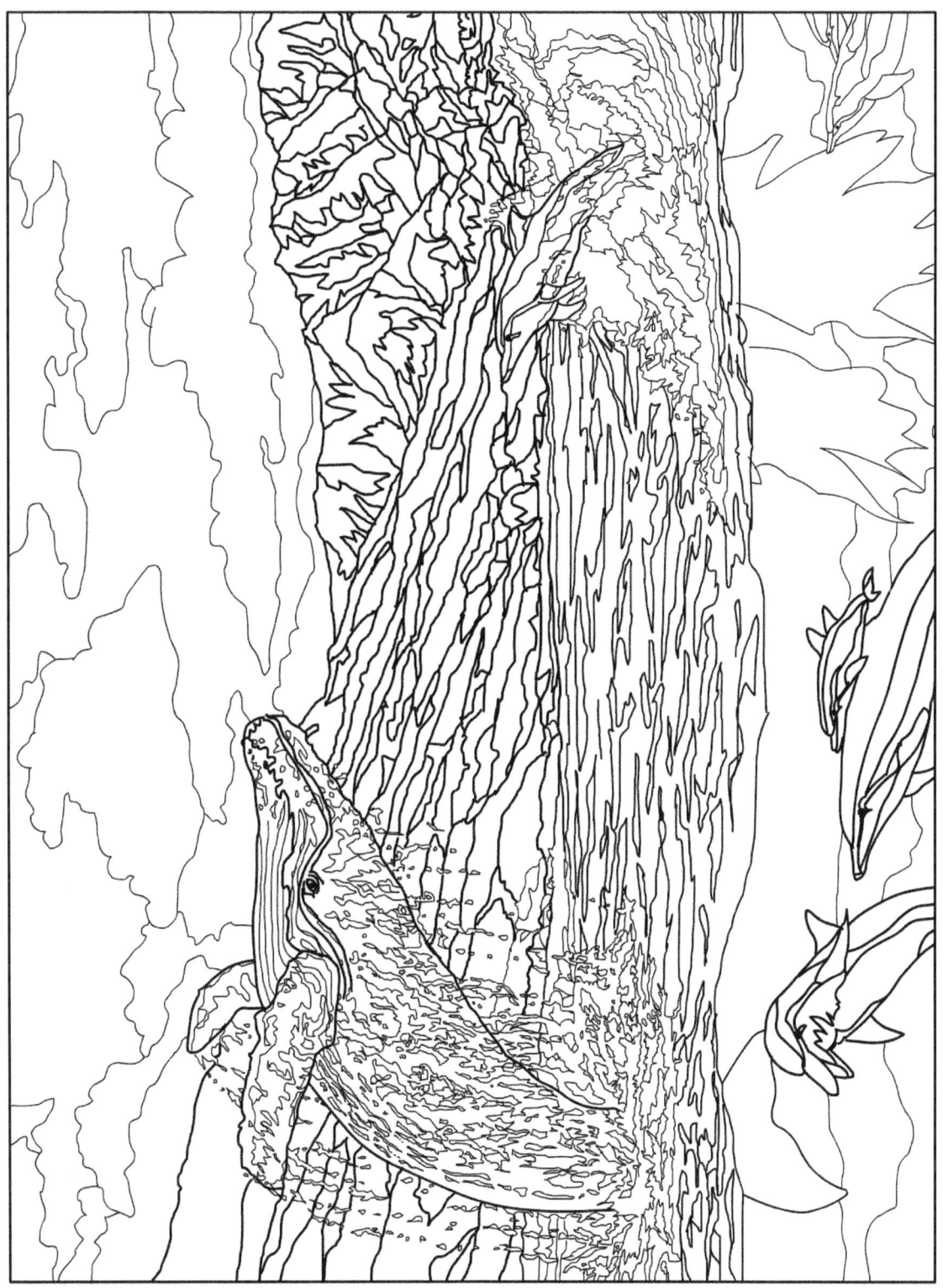

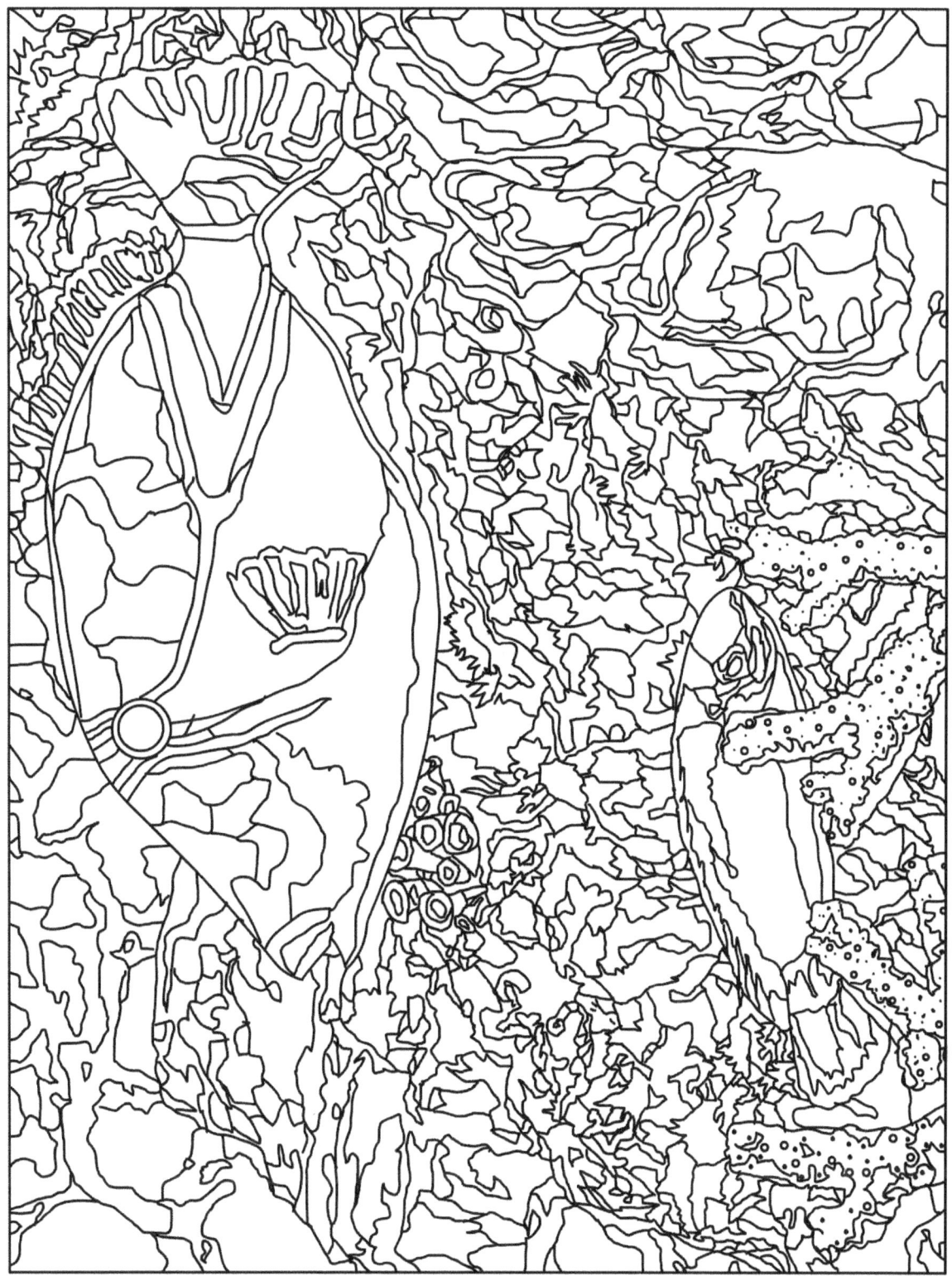

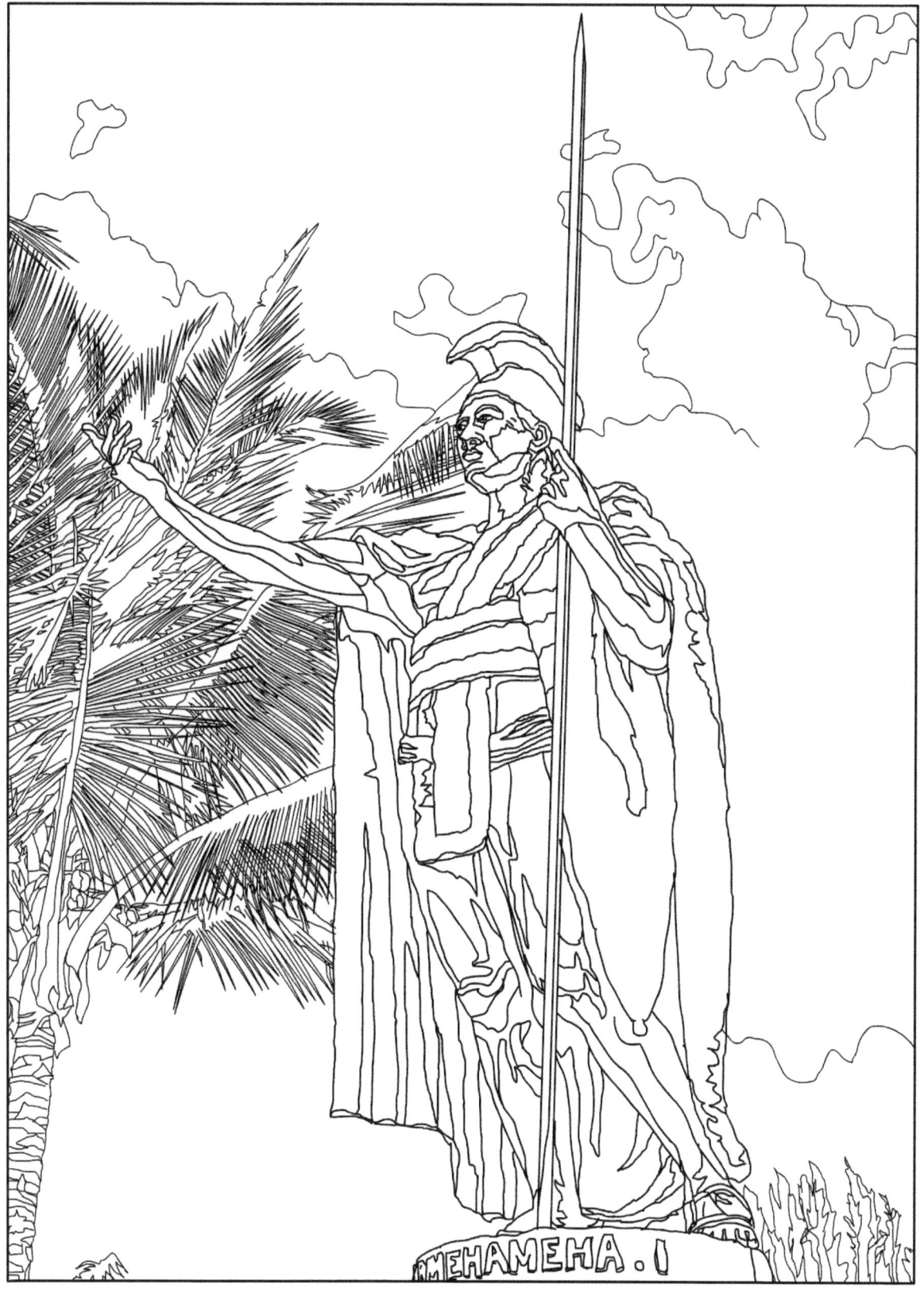

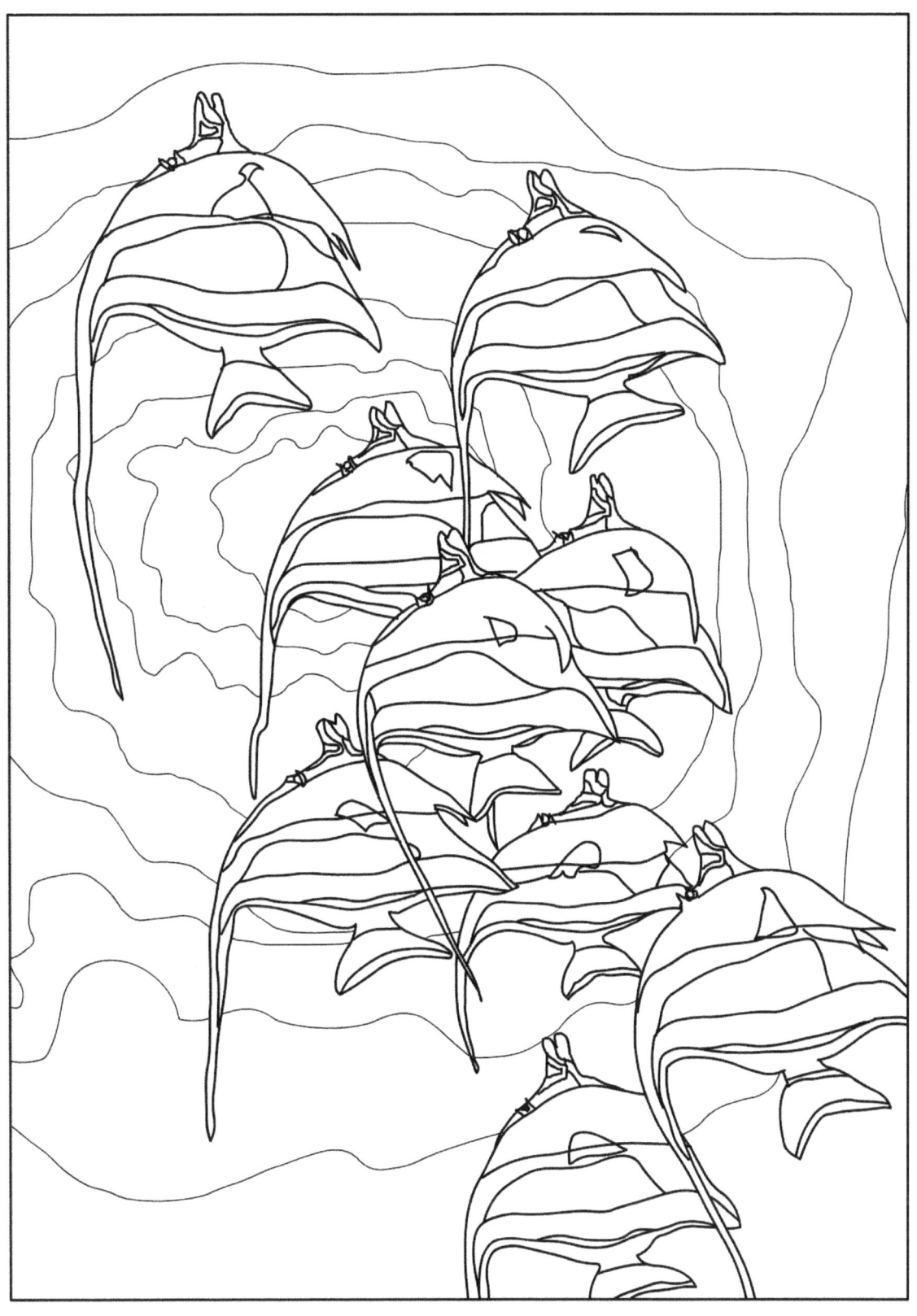

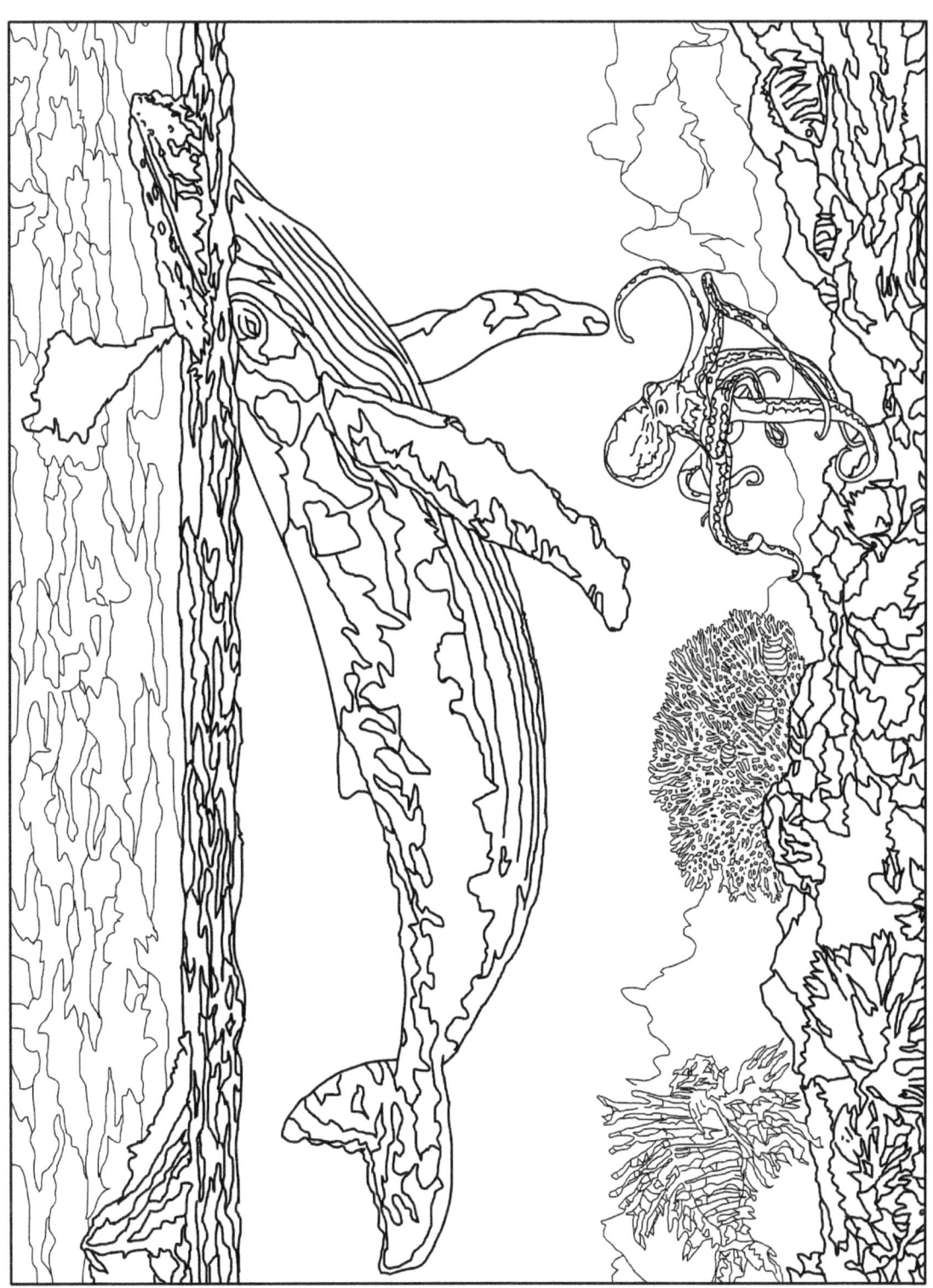

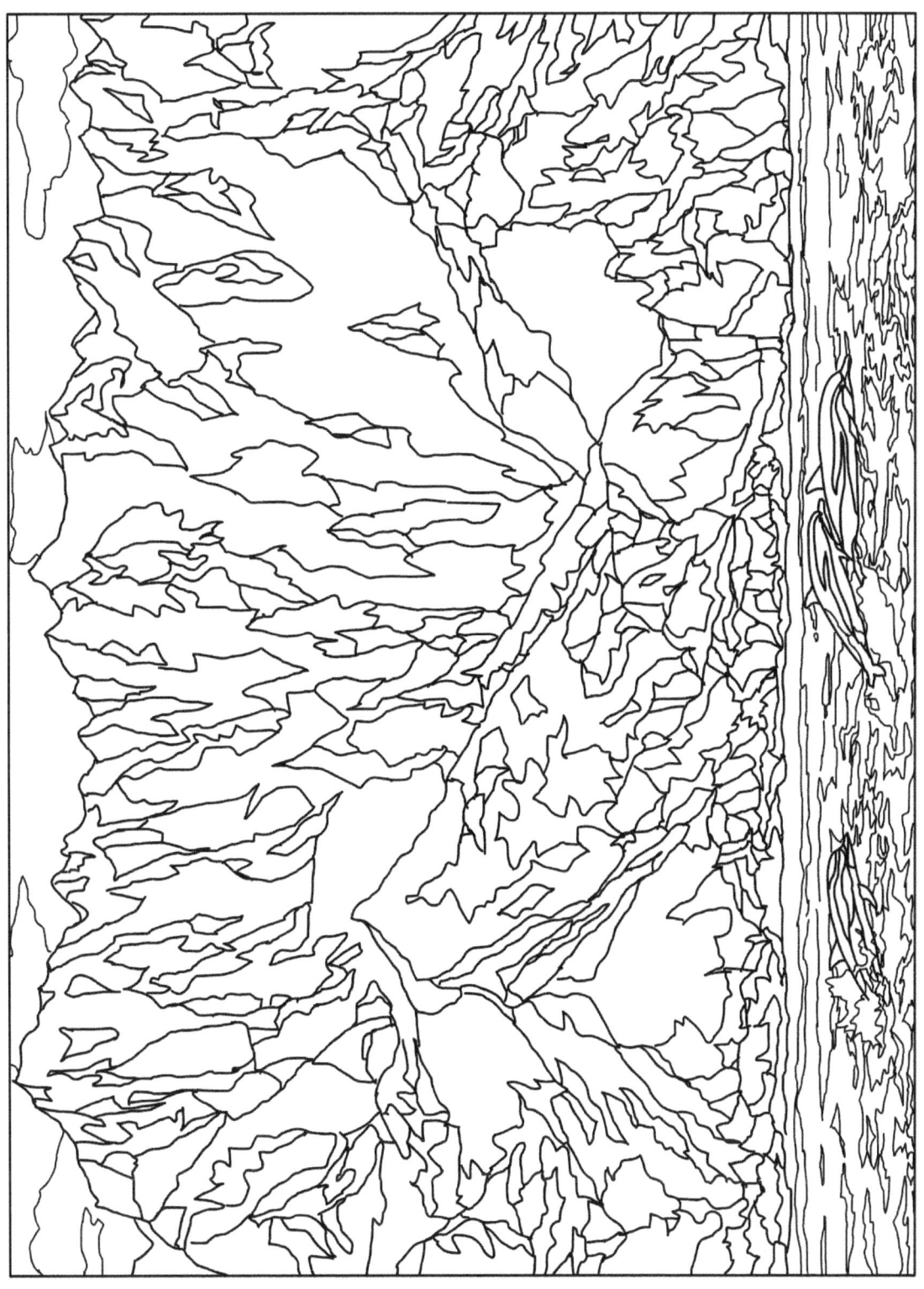

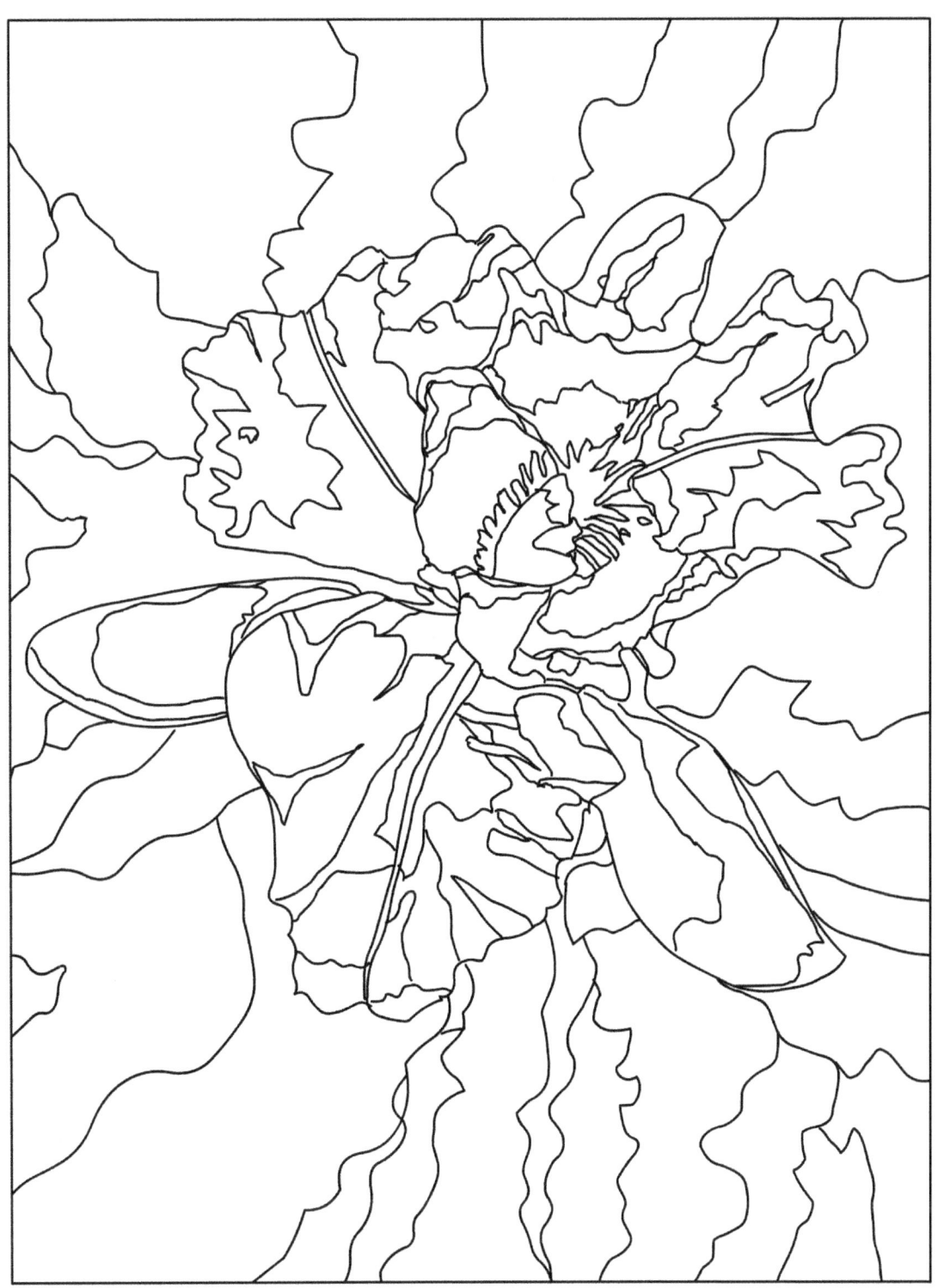

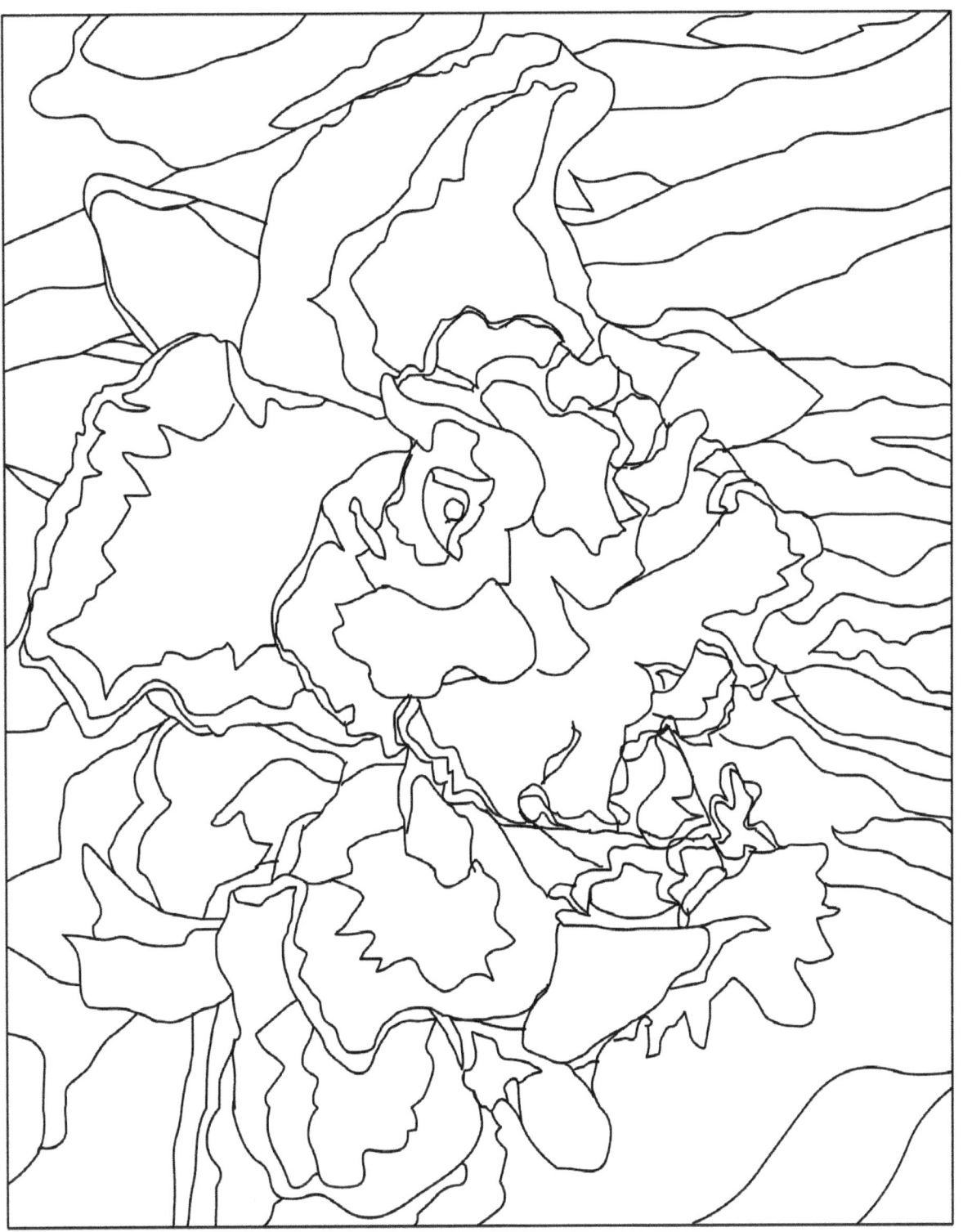

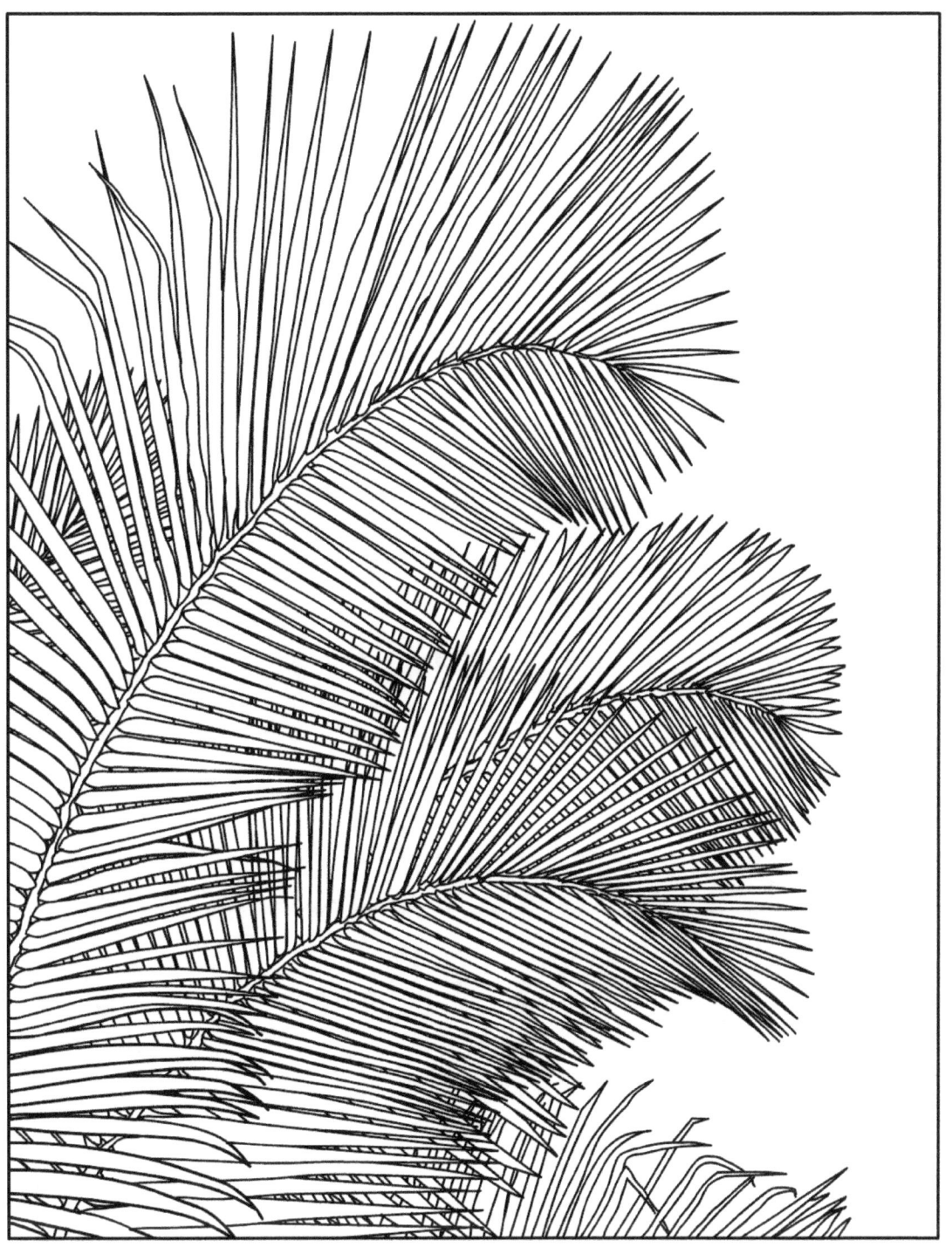

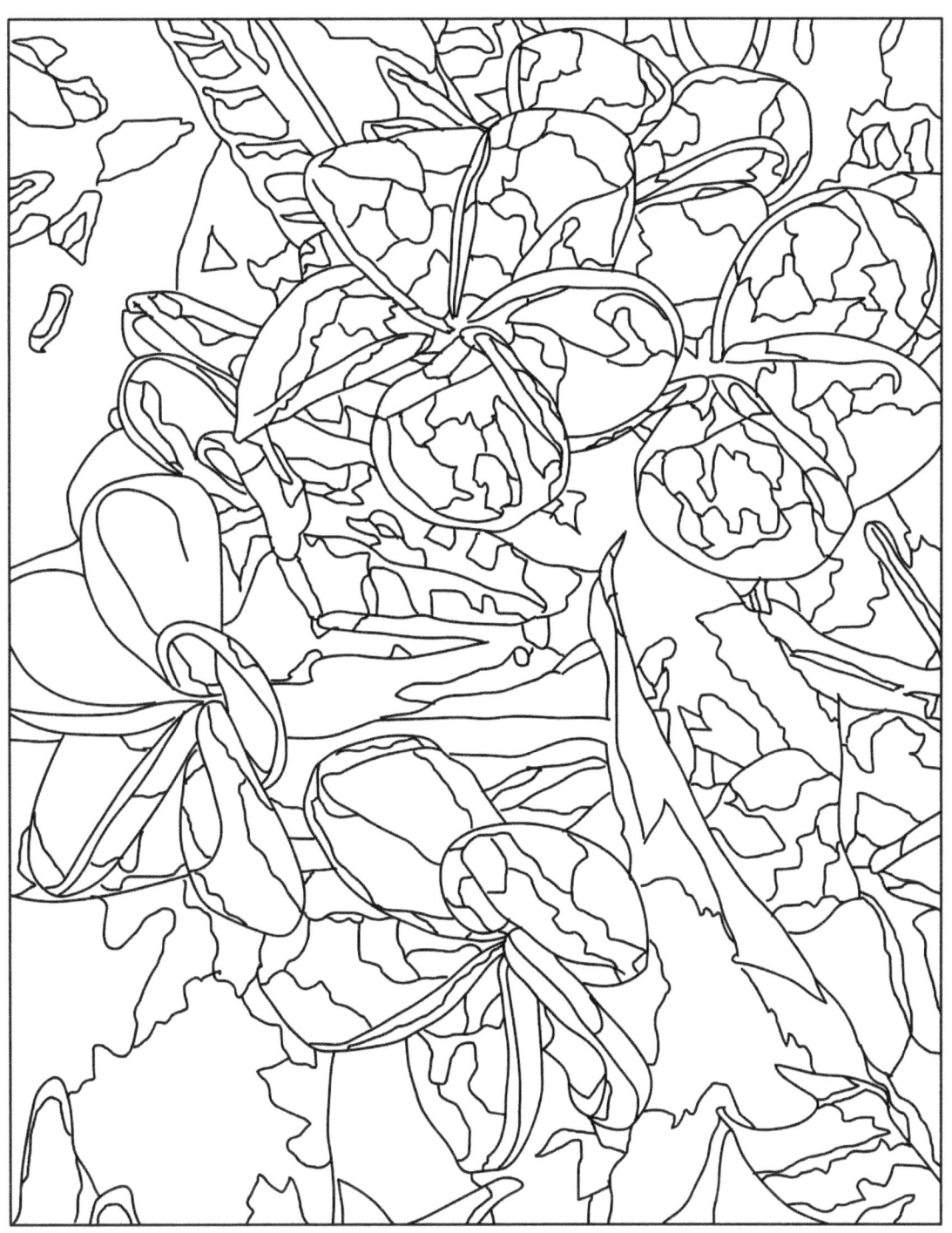

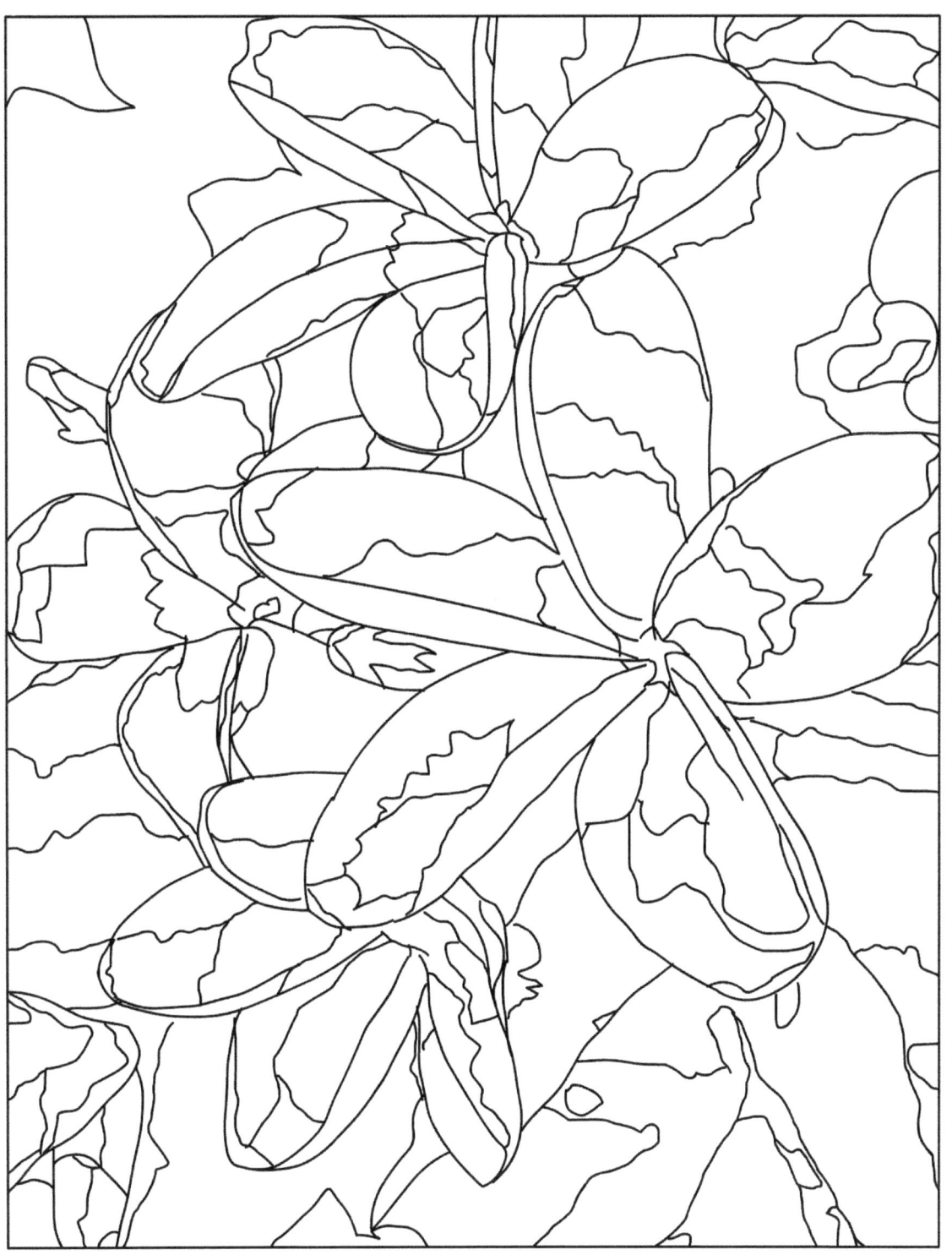

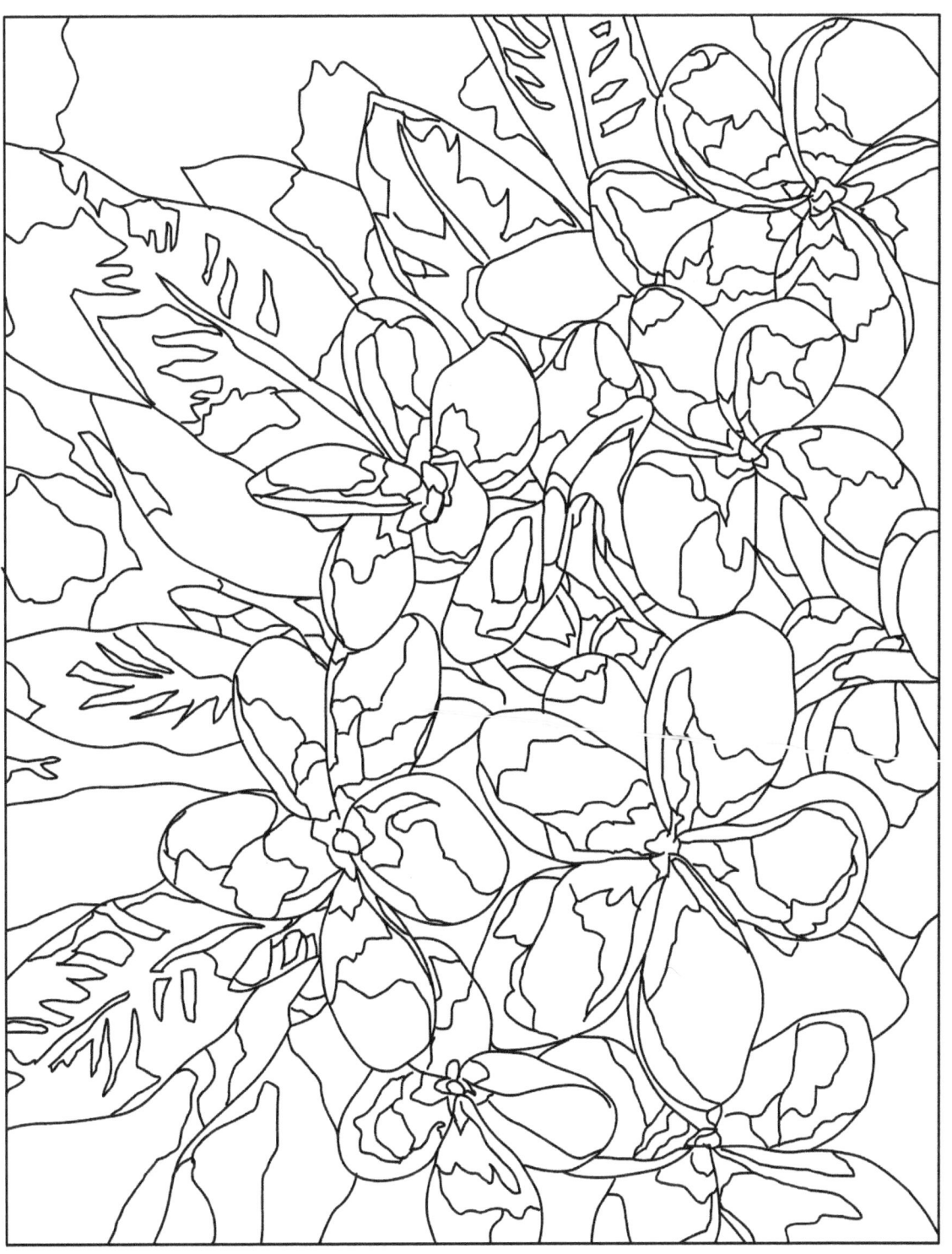

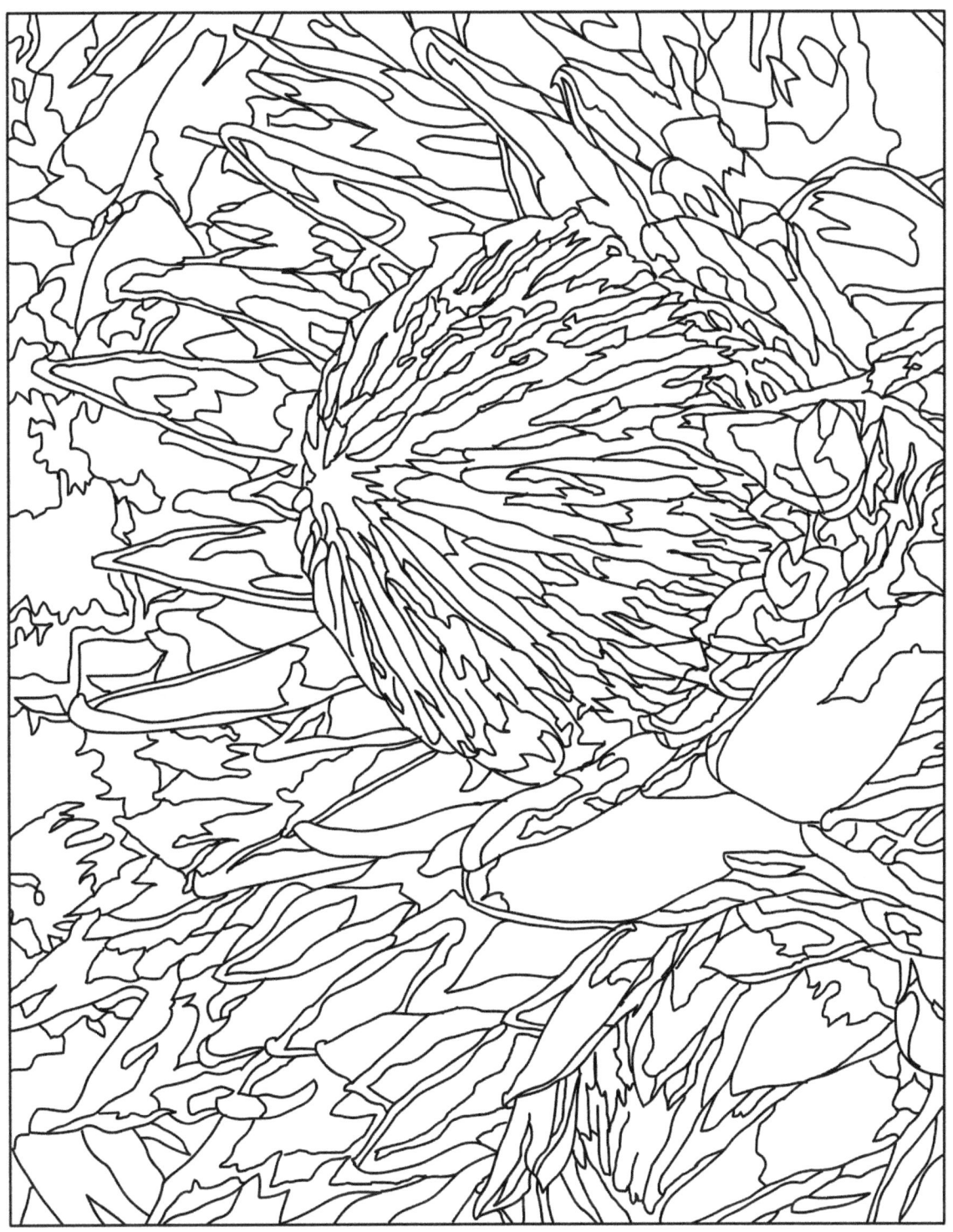

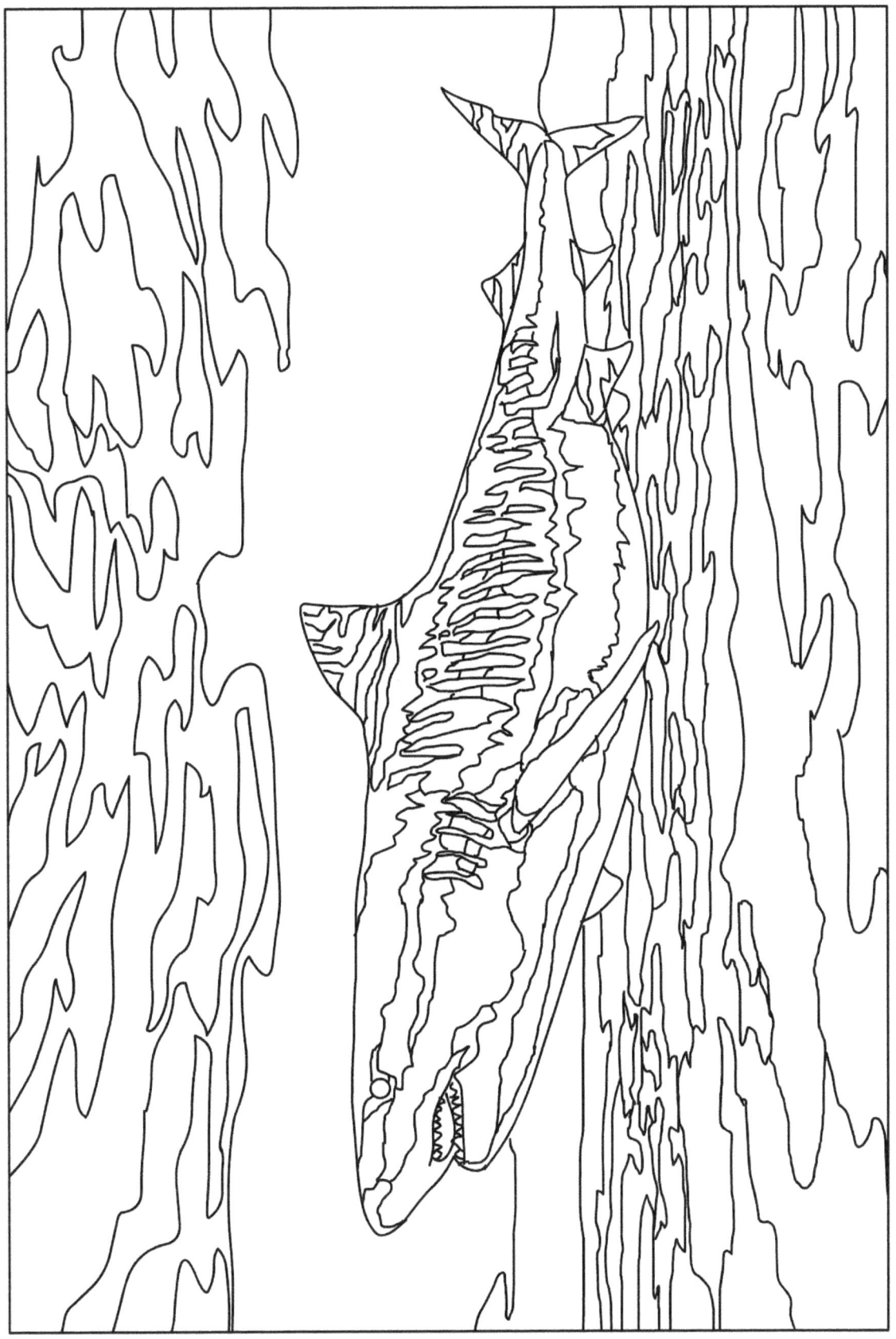

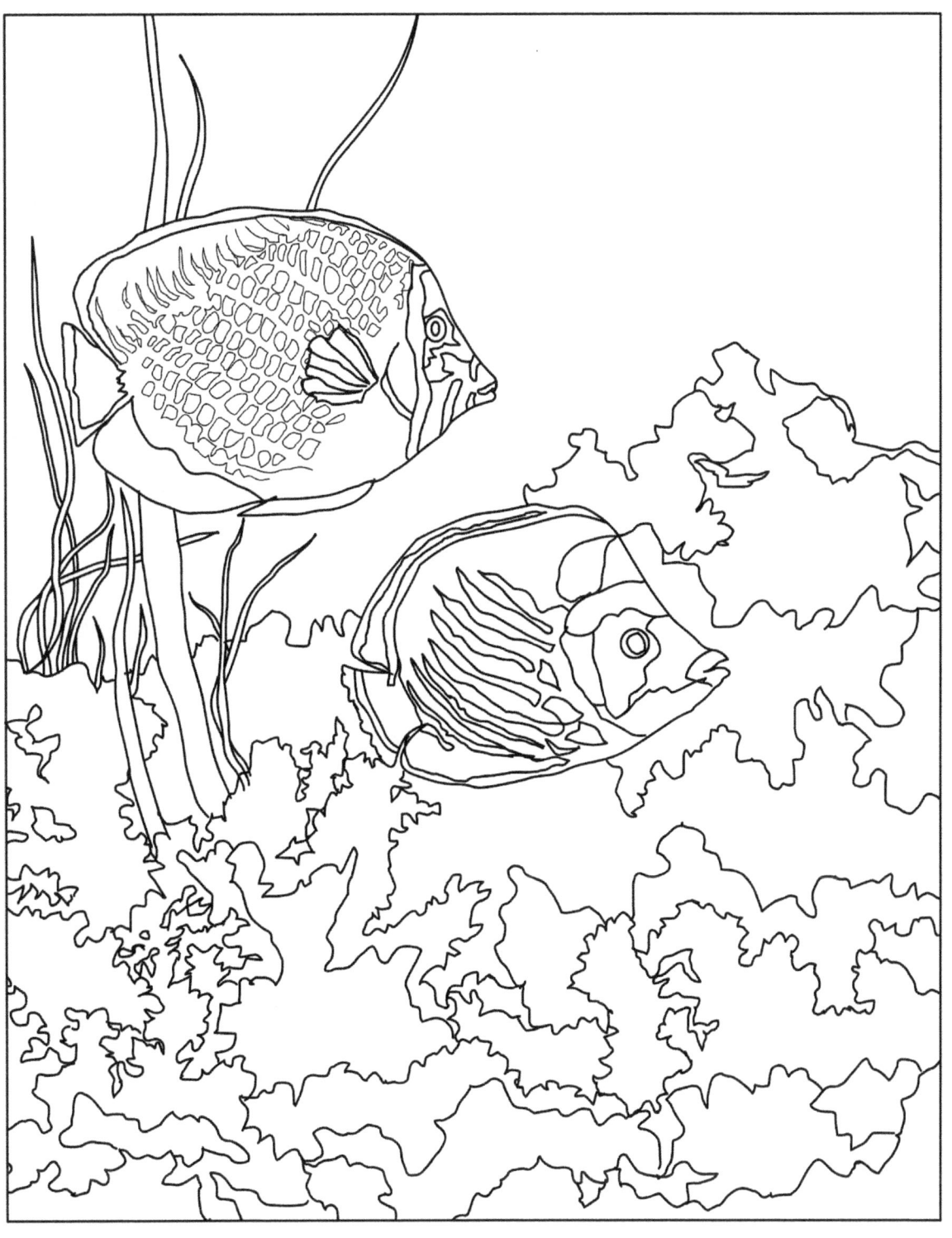

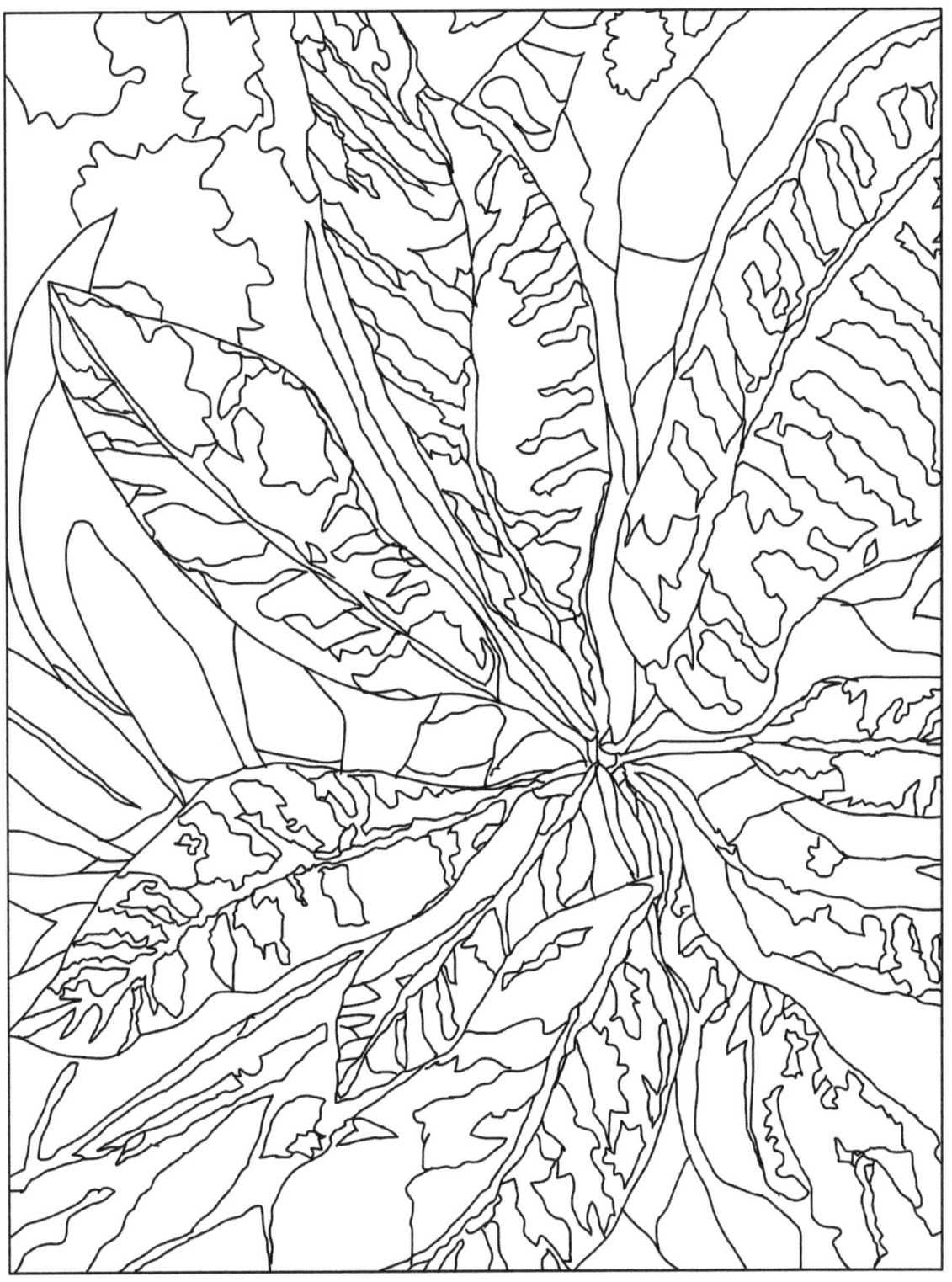

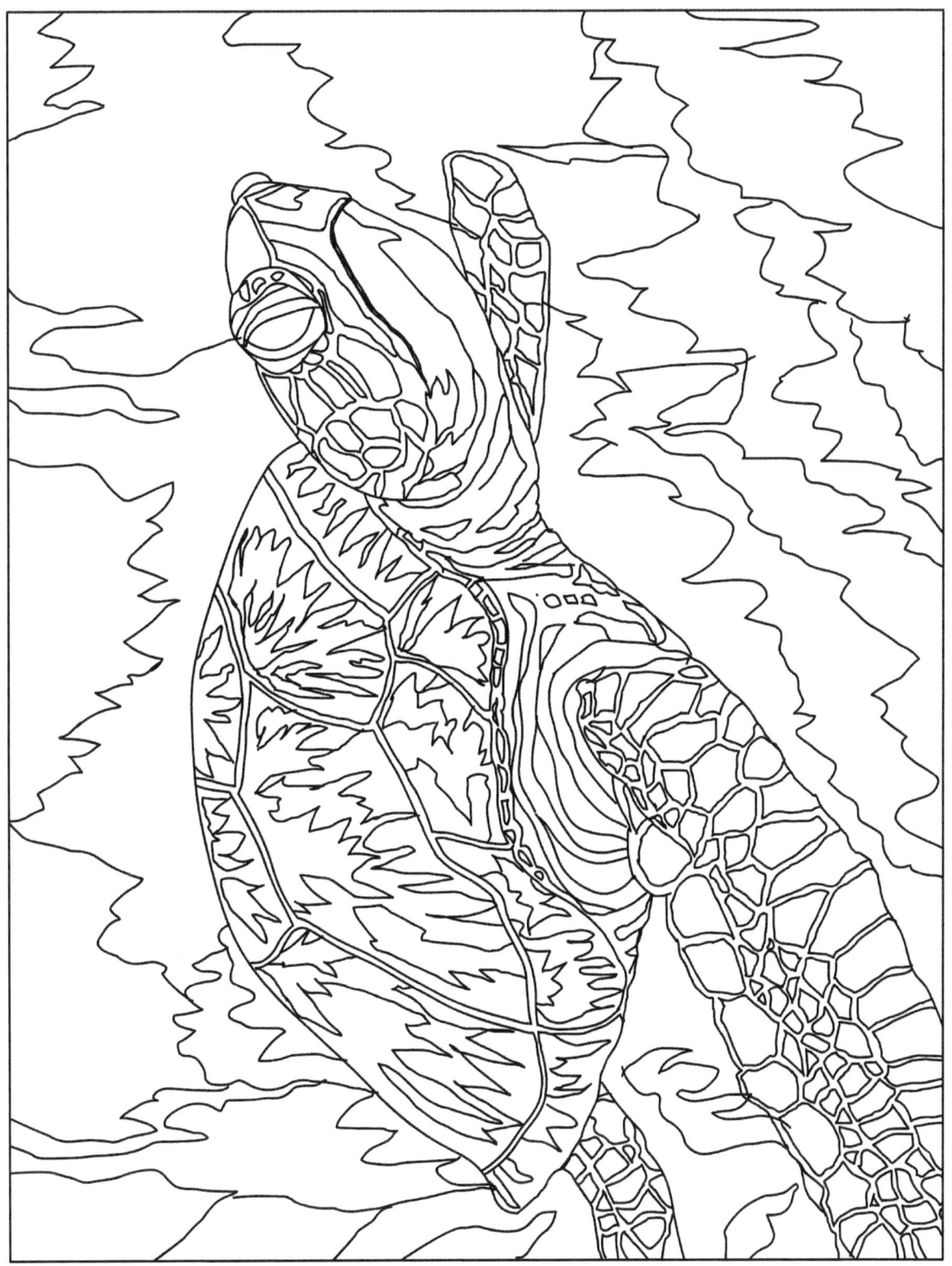

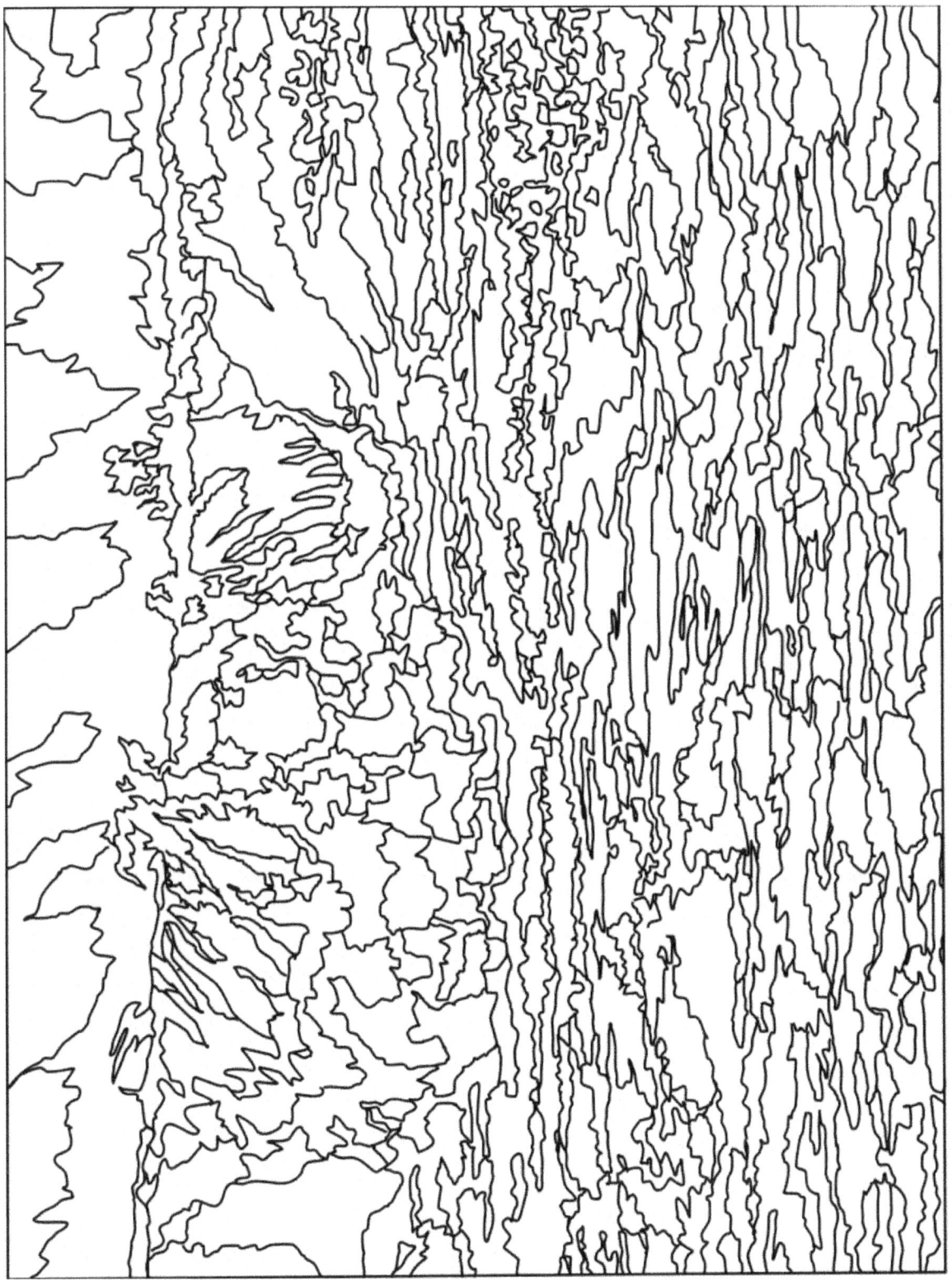

I have over a hundred large Hawaiian canvas prints and paintings, and nearly 200 smaller watercolor/prints at my Etsy art site. The coloring book pages are based on some of these. If you like my Hawaiian art, check these out at hawaiiseascapes.etsy.com

Check out my other books at Amazon. I have these books currently published:

 Creation of the Universe and Other Strange Mormon Beliefs Revealed. (A church member tells all the Secrets the Authorities Don't Want to Talk About.)

 How to Import From China Starting With $250 and Make a Small Fortune!

 How To Use Your Money Making Genes to Become a Success and Make a Small Fortune.

 How to Publish Books on Amazon Kindle and Make a Small Fortune, The E-Book Money Making System

        Thanks....

www.ingramcontent.com/pod-product-compliance
Lightning Source LLC
Chambersburg PA
CBHW080550190526
45169CB00007B/2706